Betta
Care

T.F.H. Publications
One TFH Plaza
Third and Union Avenues
Neptune City, NJ 07753

This book has been published with the intent to provide accurate and authoritative information in regard to the subject matter within. While every precaution has been taken in preparation of this book, the publisher and author assume no responsibility for errors or omissions. Neither is any liability assumed for damages resulting from the use of the information herein.

ISBN 0-7938-1040-X

www.tfh.com

Table
of Contents

Personality &
A Fighting Urge

The Most Beautiful Aquarium Fish

If how long it's been in the tropical fish hobby is any measure of a fish's popularity, then bettas are by far one of the most popular aquarium fishes ever known. A number of different hobby fishes are just about as beautiful as some of today's highly domesticated bettas, but few have had the long-term popularity of *Betta splendens*, a fish known simply as the betta or by some as the Siamese fighting fish.

The name Siamese fighting fish is well earned by this pugilist, but this has not thwarted the enthusiasm of hobbyists who keep them. Male bettas instinctively fight with one another, and in the aquarium, where the weaker ones cannot escape as they usually can in the wild, only the strong survive. Although males fight viciously among themselves, one male in a community tank rarely bothers other species present, certainly a contributing factor to the betta's great popularity. As you might expect with such a pugnacious fish, males are quite brutal toward females, even those in spawning condition. Females, like males, tend to fight among themselves, but not nearly as intensively as males.

Regardless of color or shape, the Siamese fighting fish or betta is formally known as Betta splendens.

The brilliant colors and fantastic finnage of male bettas have made them outstanding fish in the aquarium hobby for almost a century.

It would seem that all of these behavioral problems would cause the betta to take the route to oblivion traveled by so many other aggressive fishes that have had a fleeting popularity in the aquarium hobby. However, bettas have become, as a result of many decades of domestication and selective breeding, one of the most spectacularly beautiful fish the hobby has ever known. Probably because of that beauty, bettas have remained popular in the hobby almost since its inception. It also helps that single males kept in small containers become very responsive to their owner and are close to being true pets.

Records show that modern-day bettas owe a major part of their good looks to Asian breeders who over a century ago began to dedicate themselves to developing long finnage and brilliant colors in an otherwise unspectacular fish. As with the domestication and culture

Put two male bettas together and you will have a fight, complete with ripped fins and possibly torn jaws and missing scales.

of goldfish, Asian families devoted all their efforts for generations to producing the ancestors of today's long-finned, brilliant bettas. So highly developed are the bettas of today's aquarium hobby that few beginning hobbyists, given the opportunity, would be able to recognize a wild betta as the same species.

To Fight or Not to Fight

If you put two male bettas in one container, they will fight, resulting in torn fins and lost scales. These could easily fungus or one male could become stressed. If you want your male to live a long life, keep it away from other males.

Fighting

Ounce for ounce, the male betta is a far tougher adversary than most fishes, but this pugnacity is aimed at only one species—his own. Some people find this difficult to comprehend. In reality, the betta is so indifferent to most other fishes that there is a feeling among some that a mistake was made when it was called the "fighting fish."

In a community aquarium, the betta is likely to be picked on. Some fish will nudge it along to get it going. Others find its long fins a good target for an occasional nip. This is why bettas should be separated not only from their brothers but from almost all other fishes as well. A male betta will not only fight other males but also will flare up and try to fight his own reflection in a mirror. Even a painted wooden dummy crudely carved to resemble a betta will arouse his wrath.

Why do these fish like to fight? No one can explain it. The fighting instinct does not first appear in a fully mature male as you might think. It first appears in youngsters only eight or nine weeks old. As the young fish develop, little mock battles ensue. The fish, not even an inch long, circle each other head to tail with all of their fins

A single male betta (or several females) can be kept in a community tank because bettas do not fight outside their species.

extended and mouths open. Each seems to want the other to knock a chip off his shoulder. Sometimes there is a quick ripping motion and the skirmish is over.

History

The first living Siamese fighting fish were introduced into Germany in 1896, but they did not arrive in the United States until 1910. William T. Innes, an American originator of the aquarium hobby, stated that in the early days of the hobby the "original" *Betta splendens* had a yellowish brown body with a few indistinct horizontal lines. At moments of emotional stress, the male darkened and showed metallic green scales. The dorsal fin also was this color, tipped with red, while the anal fin was red, tipped with blue. The ventrals then were, as they are now, red tipped with white. Fins were of moderate size, and there was a rounded tail to match.

It was not until 1927 that the first brightly colored, flowing finned Siamese fighting fish as we know them today arrived in the United States, consigned to dealer Frank Locke of San Francisco. He noted both dark-bodied and light-bodied specimens in the shipment and thought the light-bodied fish were a new species he called *Betta cambodia*. It soon became apparent that the light fish were just a variant of the single species. It later was suggested that the Cambodian strain (light body with brightly colored fins)

Female and immature bettas generally lack bright colors, often have two stripes on the sides or vertical bars, and do not have long fins.

Colored females now are produced in some color varieties, but they lack the finnage and attitude of the male.

Personality & A Fighting Urge

originated in French Indochina (current Southeast Asia) about 1900.

Classification

Siamese fighting fish are one of many species belonging to the large group of fishes known as the Anabantoidei. Like other fishes belonging to this "air-breathing" group, they are often referred to as anabantoids or (incorrectly) as anabantids. All anabantoids have at least one anatomical feature in common that is lacking in most other fishes and is critical to their very survival: They are equipped with an accessory air-breathing organ known as the suprabranchial organ or "labyrinth." This organ allows them to survive in water that contains a very low concentration of dissolved oxygen. They can take in atmospheric air through the mouth when coming to the surface and pass it over the labyrinth organ located at the bases of the gills. There the oxygen is extracted from the air to be used by the fish. Anabantoids often are referred to as labyrinth fishes, and most are known as gouramis.

The genus *Betta* itself is a large and complicated one restricted to tropical southeastern Asia into Indonesia, with at least 40 to 45 species currently recognized. Many tiny but colorful species of *Betta* recently have been described from isolated swamps and islands in Malaysia and Borneo, and some of these have entered the aquarium hobby as rarities greatly sought by specialists. *Betta splendens* has

Go For Single Colors

Advanced betta keepers prefer males of single colors to those showing two or three colors on their bodies and fins. The ultimate goal of betta breeders is a fish of a single pure color. Cambodians or butterfly bettas, recognized by different body and fin colors, are of course exceptions. If possible, try to buy and breed fish of the purest colors available to you.

Solid colors rule the lives of betta specialists. Deep brown, almost black, specimens such as this make a keeper's heart beat faster.

been used as the scientific name for the Siamese fighting fish since 1910, but some ichthyologists (scientists who study fishes) believe this name will eventually be changed.

Most species of *Betta* are rather elongated fishes with straight, nearly parallel upper and lower edges of the body, the dorsal fin much shorter at the base than the anal fin, and with 25 to 30 scales along the middle of the side. Species range from about an inch long to over 4 inches, with *Betta splendens* at the upper part of this range. The species of *Betta* are notoriously difficult to identify, so many species are based mostly on color characters as seen in living speci-

mens. Some species of betta build floating nests of air bubbles (bubblenesters) to hold the eggs, while others pick the eggs from the bottom and incubate them in the mouth (mouthbrooders). The Siamese fighting fish is a bubblenesting species.

Mixed colors have their followers, but most complicated patterns produce a large number of unsuitable culls when bred, making the life of the breeder harder.

A beautiful iridescent blue double-tail is the result of selective breeding from chance mutations.

Buying Bettas

The betta has undergone a great transformation since it was first kept as an aquatic pet. The resemblance to the wild fish in form and coloration is slight, at least in males where the finnage has been bred to lengths resembling flowing drapery. Colors have been sorted out until we have males (and sometimes females) of single solid colors, and the colors have been greatly intensified. Over the past decades colors and finnage have been modified greatly, perhaps more than could be imagined even by most breeders. Since bettas are one of the easiest egglayers to breed, they offer a breeder great potential for color breeding through selection from among the many offspring of controlled matings. Because females of most strains are generally similar and not very colorful, selection usually is done through the males.

Male bettas can be found in many spectacular colors. Females tend to have drab coloring.

Most pet shops carrying tropical fish offer bettas for sale. When looking over the offerings, be discriminating and shop around. However, don't discount your esthetic reaction to a particular fish—trust your reactions to general proportions, purity of colors, mixture or distribution of colors, beauty and condition of the fins, and general demeanor.

Joining In

There are hundreds of aquarium clubs in the U.S. and Europe and many local betta clubs. The International Betta Congress (IBC) unites betta fanciers on a worldwide scale and can quickly bring a novice betta fancier up to date on what is going on in bettas. The IBC operates a web site at: ibc.bettas.org/.

How Long Will My Betta Live?

Most betta enthusiasts are of the opinion that bettas have an expected life of about 30 months. This is why it is important to purchase young fish if you wish to spawn them and enjoy them for more than a few months. Of course, such averages reflect extremes, and information from several sources indicates that bettas can live much longer. Under laboratory conditions, males have been found to live for at least nine years. Each of these fish was given a tank of several gallons all to itself and was exercised each day by being chased around the tank by a researcher. Room and exercise may be the keys to longer lives.

When purchasing bettas, try to find out the age of the fish you want to take home. Young specimens between five and eight months old are in their prime for breeding, which makes them very desirable. Sadly, many of us succumb to showy, fully grown specimens that already are old and will be with us for only a short time. The younger fish will be with us longer, and it is enjoyable to watch the fish grow and change with time. With proper care, a betta can give much pleasure for a year or two.

Young specimens are better potential breeders than older ones and will be available for breeding longer. Younger fish usually also have more vigor, and they show it. They tend to be more active and aggressive. Individuals just over three months old have on occasion produced good spawns. Fish over a year in age become less active and tend to be inactive for long periods of time. Look for activity if the age of the fish is in question. The presence of a nest can be an indicator of youth but is not a surefire sign and cannot be taken as a positive indicator of ability or inclination to spawn. If the fish appears to be willing to fight his neighbor he may be a good candidate for purchase.

Pour, Don't Net

It is best to move betta fry by catching them in a cup or glass and carefully pouring them into the new container rather than trying to catch them in a net, which could cause severe damage.

The most successful way to obtain fish of a particular age is to get them from the breeder or his agent. However, often a good fish from an unknown source can be obtained from a pet shop. Most of these come from the Orient, where fish farms produce hundreds of thousands of bettas yearly. Although most of these are quite commonly colored and formed, the experienced eye can on occasion find an exceptional fish for breeding purposes.

Occasionally young "unsexed" bettas will be offered for sale. Look for the most obviously healthy, active, and aggressive youngsters. Color should be a secondary consideration unless you are looking for a particular color. Do not sacrifice vigor for color. If the unsexed fish seem to be of good proportions, finnage, and demeanor, as well as color, they will, if given good conditions, give much pleasure as they grow, and they will be ready for spawning in a very short time. Knowing the fish's age will be helpful. Some breeders feel that bettas are most ready for breeding at six months of age, but bettas just three months old have been bred successfully. It might be that most breeders wait too long to start breeding their fish. There is some evidence that if bettas are kept from spawning for long periods they show more reluctance or inability to spawn. Conversely, bettas that have been spawned periodically prove to be excellent spawners.

Fancy Bettas: Finnage & Colors

Finnage

Bettas bear a variety of fins that are important in evaluating the desirability of a specimen. The dorsal fin is the short-based fin on the back, the caudal fin is the tail fin, and the anal fin is the long-based fin that runs along the lower edge of the body. Behind the gill covers are the pectoral fins, which vary little in bettas, but under the throat are the ventral or pelvic fins that often are elongated and colored in males. Each fin is made from thick fin rays separated by thin membranes; small spines precede the dorsal and anal fins.

Fullness of fins as well as length of fins are most desirable. Long but narrow fins, for instance, can indicate poor stock or poor rearing

In the best double-tails the caudal fin development is echoed in longer dorsal and anal fins as well.

conditions. Long fins are desirable, but fullness indicates a better fish. Look for a roundness of the caudal and anal fins that extends from just behind the ventral fins so the anal fin seems to meld with the caudal. Look for abrupt changes in direction in the fin rays; they might indicate that the fins at one time were damaged or diseased. Look for a very light or very dark edge to the fins, as this very often will indicate that the fins still have some growing to do. Fin rays that extend just beyond the growing edge of the fin seem to indicate good, robust stock. A folding or draping effect in the fins, sometimes even when spread out, indicates good stock. A ragged appearance to the fins is undesirable. It might be best to also reject any fish that seems unable to carry their finnage.

The most commonly seen caudal fin form is the "veiltail" or melon-shaped caudal, though other shapes such as "roundtail" are becoming increasingly popular. Other forms for the caudal include the "pintail" or pointed form and also the "delta" or triangular form. The delta form seems to be especially elusive in bettas; it is spread toward the edges of the fin and more or less squared-off at the outer edge. Some breeders see advantages in recognizing extensions of the fin rays, referring to "combtail" or "fringetail" bettas.

Double-tails

In addition to color versatility, the betta has experienced changes in form as well. Bettas with two tails now are widely available. The caudal fins are truly two in number and are arranged one above the other. Thus far, the tails do not equal the fullness or beauty of the single-tailed fish, but the potential of these fish some day will be exploited by an adventurous breeder and the double-tails will rival the single-tails and be as attractive and sought-after as the varieties of fancy goldfish with multilobed caudals.

Double-tailed bettas also possess an attribute that offers much potential: The dorsal fin is about twice as wide at the base as that of the usual betta, starting much closer to the head, and has almost twice the num-

Compare the rounded tail of the fish at the bottom with the double tail of the male above it. Neither fish is more attractive than the other, they just represent two very different varieties.

ber of rays as the usual dorsal fin. The dorsal is as wide as the anal fin and almost as long. First impressions suggest that the fish might be swimming upside-down. It is a credit to the species when *Betta splendens* is readily available in many color combinations with the very large dorsal fins and double tails, very wide and long, flowing one over the other as the fish swims. Beautifully colored and formed double-tailed bettas in yellow, bronze, black, red, blue, and green have been seen. The truth is, however, that these very beautiful fish often are not selectively bred, which means that the particular color and/or form aberration is lost until it accidentally shows up again.

Proportions

The proportions of the body relative to the fins are very important. A large-bodied fish with relatively short fins will most likely not develop long fins. In fact, these males can sometimes be mistaken for females because of their short fins, and they have caused hobbyists some real consternation when set up to spawn with other males! Occasionally these males will be true throwbacks to the wild form but possess more sophisticated coloring.

A very slim-bodied fish with seemingly good fins may be exhibiting the results of disease, poor inheritance, or dietary or other environmental deficiencies. It is difficult to say just what ideal proportions might be, but an extremely slim body is to be avoided.

Color

Color is pretty much a matter of taste, so not too much can be said about what you should select—but a few suggestions can be made as to how you might select for color. Most of the bettas on the market possess more than one color distributed quite randomly. They are usually very nice fish and make worthy additions to community tanks. However, if you are interested in breeding for solid colors, it is worth the time and effort to seek out individuals that are decidedly one color in body and fins or nearly so, for if you start with breeders of mixed colors you are set back immeasurably.

This male may be carrying excessive finnage for its body, not a favored trait among specialist keepers.

Some relatively recent varieties of bettas include those with dark bodies and lighter colored fins. Examples are blacks or browns with yellow fins. They have become known as bi-colored bettas. Another bi-colored betta, the Cambodian betta, has been with us for many years. It has a light pink body that can be combined with red, blue, or green fins, and its versatility can be carried on further to include Cambodians with black, yellow, or white fins.

Such versatility of color is possible not only in a given group of bettas but even in a single spawning when spawning for a particular color pattern. One of the great joys of working with this fish is to be surprised with the outcome of a particular color spawning for the subtle variety to be found in the fry.

Cambodians with almost colorless bodies and brilliant fins are among the most attractive bettas but are difficult to breed consistently.

Yellow, red, black, and blue bettas exist because selective breeding has produced them. Yellow, red, black, and blue have been found to be the basic cell colors in bettas. Selective breeding has altered and intensified the distribution of the desired color cells while diminishing or inhibiting the others, thus creating "pure" color strains. Non-discriminating breeding of bettas produces the randomly colored mixes we see so often.

Carrying Fins

To be attractive, a betta with long, flowing fins must be large enough and strong enough to carry his fins in an erect manner and be able to move freely. Some long-finned bettas have bodies that are too small or weak to allow them to handle their fins, and any water currents in the container easily stress them.

On rare occasions you will find a betta that appears to have extremely strong coloring that is all pervading, quite even, and with much depth. This is true in reds, greens, and blues. In fact, these individuals often seem to be so "full of color" that even the pectorals are brightly colored. The pectoral fins in most bettas are clear and not showy, but in these highly colored individuals the constant motion of these fins is easily observable. This is a characteristic well worth working for.

The following descriptions of colors are given to suggest how variable colors are in bettas. It is not suggested that the following list is complete, as new varieties are coming along all the time. Those

This betta probably would never win an award, but the symmetry of the fin pattern in this (probably female) Cambodian certainly is attractive.

listed below can be spawned with a good degree of predictability from fish exhibiting or carrying the required color or color pattern.

Reds

Solid red or candy apple red coloring has a clarity and depth that make it one of the most brilliant reds you can expect to see in bettas. Solid red bettas often have red pectoral fins.

Varying amounts of black pigment cells produce blood reds, tomato reds, and maroons. These reds can be quite velvety in appearance. Darker reds often have concentrations of black cells edging the scales. A further intensification of black cells over red can be produced by selective breeding, and the result can be a very dark-bodied fish with red fins. Such fish have been produced and named "firefins."

Red bettas come in several shades, but some are extremely metallic and even have bright red pectoral fins. The color is found in all finnage varieties.

Quick & Easy Betta Care

A close look at a colorful betta shows the pigment cells that together produce the reds, yellows, and blacks so valued in bettas.

A red-violet can also be spawned, given the proper breeders. It is a red with a very evenly distributed coating of blue cells over the red.

Blues

There are basically two blues, dark blue and steel blue, in bettas.

Selective Breeding

By breeding only males carrying a desired color or fin character, betta breeders select for that color or finnage. They start with the purest lines possible, males that seldom produce other colors or fin types, and eliminate the offspring that are not up to their standards. If you breed your bettas for a specific character, always start off with parents that already show that character.

Dark blue (sometimes referred to as cornflower blue or royal blue) is a deep basic blue that can tend toward a blue-purple. This is a tricky color to work with. When blue is mated to blue, only a portion of the fry will be blue like the parents. The rest will be divided between steel blue or green. This is due to a partial dominance in blues. A spawning of steel blue and green will produce all dark blues.

Steel blue is basically a deep blue with an overall silvery sheen. The fins are quite silvery too. It has also been known as gunmetal blue. A mating of steel blue to steel blue will produce steel blue.

Greens

Geneticists tell us that the iridescent green color in bettas is produced by waste products of metabolism and that the "iridocytes" (the cells that produce the green color) are crystalline in form. A general term for such cells is guanophores. They also tell us that blue is transmitted to our eyes by the same kinds of cells, but something about the structure of the cells determines whether we perceive green or blue. This is not true only in our beloved bettas but also in birds such as blue jays.

The green in bettas is a beautiful green-turquoise color with much depth; it is iridescent, reflective, and shiny. A mating of a green betta to a green betta will produce green bettas.

Cambodians

The Cambodian lacks color cells in the body. The fins of this color mutation are usually fully colored, but even this manifestation has begun to give way to those breeders who would manipulate the fish's color or color pattern.

Cambodians exhibit very sparse populations of yellow, red, black, or blue cells over a background color found to be a combination of colors of tissue, organs, and blood. Thus, the cleanest of Cambodians would possess a quite even salmon or pink-beige coloring coupled with colored fins. An intensification of any of the above-mentioned color cells will produce a Cambodian body that appears pink, reddish, pale blue, pale green, yellow, etc., coupled with fin colors mentioned.

A Cambodian betta is basically a salmon or pale pink-bodied fish that displays fin coloring in red, blue, or green. Slow to become popular with hobbyists, this color variety catches the fancy of the

The Non-Color Green

Many bettas appear to be green, and this might be considered a basic color in bettas, but actually many people do not see green but instead see shadings between turquoise and blue. The deciding factor seems to be that the green is highly iridescent, a shininess or sparkle accompanying the color. This is not true of blue bettas, even though blue is produced by the same cells (guanophores) that produce green. If green bettas are compared side by side with blue bettas, the difference is easily seen.

Mutations

A mutation is a sudden change in the chromosomes, usually caused by cosmic rays and is thus random. Mutations usually are very minor or damaging, but some have led to attractive changes in colors and finnage of bettas and other fishes. Remember that a mutation affects the chemistry of inheritance, not the character actually seen. Thus a mutation of color changes the cells that produce the color, not the color directly. Mutations are inherited, usually as recessives.

breeder because of the possibility of breeding into it the fin colors of your own choosing. The fins can be made to possess a single color, two colors, or even three colors. In one type, referred to as the "bunting," the fins are vertically banded in red, white, and blue, reminiscent of the bunting hung at political rallies. Any Cambodian coloring can, in general, be perpetuated by a spawning of like Cambodians. Cambodian is recessive to the usual colors.

Though the division of color in the fins is not very even, most keepers would call this Cambodian male a butterfly. Much better specimens often are bred.

Quick & Easy Betta Care

White bettas often are very metallic because the dark red and yellow pigments are absent or suppressed, allowing reflective white cells in the skin to show through

Blacks

The black betta has been with us a shorter time than most other colors and is not always easy to find. If you do find one, you will quickly see that the black of the black betta is not the same as the black of the black molly. Depth and intensity of the color seem to come and go as the mood of the fish changes, more so in this color than in any other. The color is at its best at the time of spawning, when it is reminiscent of a shining blue-black chunk of coal. At other times the color fades and wanes like the stripes of an angelfish. There also can be varying degrees of iridescence over the body. You might prefer to eliminate the iridescence to obtain the blackest black possible, but this is still a quite attractive variety.

Yellows

Yellow bettas can vary in the yellow range from a very pale yellow to an orange-yellow. This can be very even throughout, or the fins can

Bettas with isolated patches of color are bred and have been called marbled or piebald bettas. Unfortunately, the colors change constantly and are unpredictable.

be a paler yellow than the body. Blue or green fin bases can also enhance the color. Varying degrees of iridescence can be present on yellow bettas; iridescence makes the pattern very attractive. However, in a competitive show of bettas the most buttery yellow bettas over-all would win the trophy.

Blacks/Yellows

When you first see this combination it may be hard to accept. A

　Quick & Easy Betta Care

light body with darker fins, yes—but not the reverse. There seems to be much variance here, from a pale brown body to an almost black body. The fins can be pale beige to a buttery yellow. The yellow can also approach orange. The fins can be fully colored or translucent. They can be black-edged, which is very attractive, or possess the blue or green fin bases mentioned in the yellows. A mating of black/yellows provided a percentage of all-yellows, while a spawning of black/yellow to yellow gave an approximate 50-50 split between the colors.

These fish, as do the all-yellows, do not seem to be able to produce red pigment, which seems to be missing. They have been termed "non-reds." The non-red phenomenon has exerted a great influence on the evolution of color in bettas. The non-red gene is a known factor that has made it possible to develop greens and blues that

Betta varieties reflect a combination of random mutations that have been selectively bred and kept pure or genetically mixed with other desirable traits.

Fancy Bettas: Finnage & Colors

33

visually are greener or bluer because of the lack of red cells. Even Cambodian types have been affected. The basic yellow betta also has exerted a genetic influence. The non-red effect is to remove the betta one step further from the wild coloration, which exhibits much red. Non-red bettas, especially the blues and greens, are bluer and greener because red is not present to affect the quality of the color in the fins, in particular, and the ventral fins especially. Which fish is more desirable? One with red in the ventral fins or one without it? The instinctive answer may be one with red, but actually if a blue fish or a green fish is most desired, then one showing little or no red is most desirable.

Butterfly (Variegated)

The term "butterfly" is used to describe a pattern that is quite spectacular in bettas. It is presently applied to Cambodian, red, green, and blue-bodied strains that possess fins with colors divided more or less evenly between colored and white to clear. The fin coloring can vary greatly from almost colorless to an abrupt "painted" division of color, to an extension of color into the fin rays, giving the colored area a saw-toothed or serrated look. These patterns are very unstable in that perhaps only a quarter of a spawning may show it. The rest are commonly colored.

Clear Fins

Some individuals in the brown, yellow, and variegated strains have shown a tendency toward a lack of any color in the fins, which leaves them quite clear, almost like cellophane. Spawning for this lack of color has brought some success. The variegated strain also exhibits a tendency toward white fins as well as clear. Clear-finned bettas have been offered commercially as "cellophane bettas," which is quite apt.

Golds

The development of the gold strain was an outgrowth of the Cambodian-black cross. A few of the first generation were iridescent green, and a sparkle of gold was noted in the pectorals of some. A

There are many color variations available to Betta enthusiasts. Whatever color you choose will have no effect on the pet quality or health of the fish. Fin types and color patterns are a matter of preference.

Fancy Bettas: Finnage & Colors

Though general hobbyists seem to prefer bettas with brightly colored fins, especially in males of single colors, many specialist breeders prefer clear-finned varieties.

second generation (brother-sister matings) revealed both green and Cambodian fry that grew to possess a golden shininess over their bodies and into the primarily red fins. Pectoral fins in some were solid gold. Subsequent generations have reduced the red in the fins and enhanced the gold. An interesting sidenote is that the fry, when about two weeks to a month old, look very much like little brass nails.

Goblet &
Aquarium Care

Hardy Fish

The great majority of people who purchase bettas do so in order to add beauty and grace to their community tanks or to their divided betta tanks. Others, however, keep single male bettas in appropriate containers; many times these fish become, as close as any fish can become, pets. Bettas, being labyrinth fish, are ideal for keeping in small containers. Minimum maintenance will keep bettas in good health. They can be kept successfully in glass or plastic containers that might be assumed to be too small or confining for other tropicals and even other anabantoids such as gouramis.

Because of the existence of the labyrinth organ in bettas, many aquarists act under the assumption that these fish can safely be kept in overcrowded aquaria. They assume that because the fish get most of their oxygen from the atmosphere, keeping them in the tank will not further deplete the supply of dissolved oxygen in the water. Not only is this assumption erroneous, but it reflects poor aquarium management. Even though bettas don't use as much of the water's dissolved oxygen as other fishes of about the same weight, they do add about the same amount of water-polluting wastes to the water. Additionally, bettas are just as susceptible to diseases brought on by polluted water as are other aquarium fishes, and in the case of velvet they might be even more susceptible.

A betta can exist in a very small water space, but not for long without a water change. The smaller the water space the more often the need for a water change. A quart of water, for instance, needs changing under normal conditions at least once a week, and this seems to be about the minimum of water to be recommended. Canning jars, goldfish bowls, tumblers, snifters, candy jars, and so on can serve excellently as tiny aquaria, if the betta's environmental needs are fulfilled, which is not always easy in a small bowl. Bettas can be kept in food or canning jars, but a little imagination might suggest more interesting containers.

Any aquarist could come up with a half dozen reasons why it is better to keep bettas in larger aquaria where they will receive the correct

Fancy Tanks

Small (less than 5 gallons) vertical aquaria with five or six sides now commonly are sold in shops and do well for a single male betta, especially when used with a small pump and filter. Such tanks still must have the water changed weekly or so, and they also tend to overheat if the built-in light is left on too long.

Though living plants are not necessary for a betta to be content in a community tank, plants make an aquarium look more natural and help maintain good water conditions.

Goblet & Aquarium Care

Rows and Rows of Bowls

In many pet shops you can see dozens of pint bowls on display, each housing a brightly colored male betta. If done correctly, this is not cruel or dangerous to the betta. Pet shops tend to be warm enough for bettas, the water is changed several times a week, and the bettas are properly fed. Keeping bettas like this for a few days allows them to display beautifully and sell fast.

heating, better water conditions, and probably, a better diet. However, the reality is that many purchasers of bettas keep single males in small bowls, and this does work. Bettas require only that they be fed the proper foods regularly and sufficiently and that their

Male bettas tend to build bubblenests whenever they are near other males or females.

Quick & Easy Betta Care

Female bettas seldom have color, but they are a bit less aggressive than males. Several often can be kept together in a community aquarium.

water be kept clean. Keeping them well-fed and clean, coupled with the fact that they are labyrinth fish, makes bettas more successfully kept than goldfish in similarly sized quarters. Goldfish often succumb to oxygen deficiency in small quarters, but since bettas can obtain their needs by coming to the surface for air, they are perfectly

Singles Only

Because male bettas are so aggressive, it is best to not keep more than one male in an aquarium, even if it is very large and heavily planted. Furthermore, it may even be more hazardous keeping a male and female in the same tank, since the male may be just as antagonistic toward a female of his own kind as he is toward a male.

content in water space that would very quickly put a goldfish into oxygen distress.

Most hobbyists find that there is little difficulty in keeping several female bettas in the same aquarium if it is large enough. There may be an occasional shredded fin, but rarely do females inflict severe damage upon one another. Additionally, females are usually far less

Poor water conditions often lead to rough fin edges in male bettas and can lead to fungal infections that are hard to treat.

If you try to breed bettas, you will need to have very clean water for the young to successfully develop. Chlorine and chloramines will kill the fry.

attractive than males and torn fins are not hereditary. In most cases, maintaining perfect finnage in a female is not as important as it is in the males.

Bettas can tolerate many differences in water. A change in water need only be the same temperature, usually, as the old water, and the new water need only be aged a day to be usable. In many parts of the country the water is safe right from the tap without aging it, though letting it air to remove chlorine is always the safest precaution. If the water has been tested and found to be extremely hard or acidic, conditioners may be necessary. Bettas can tolerate much, but they can be thrown into shock and killed if a water change is too extreme.

Goblet & Aquarium Care

Sponge Filters

Pet shops sell small, simple filters that work well in just a quart or two of water. These sponge filters consist of a cube of foam over a plastic tube and are run by a small air pump. Sponge filters are inexpensive, easy to clean, and make betta maintenance easier.

Water need not be filtered when bettas are kept singly in small containers, but filtering does lengthen time periods between needed water changes. Small filters are available for small containers. A lessening of activity can indicate that the fish needs a water change. An increase of activity is noted when water is changed. Air stones are not needed for bettas. Gravel, plants, and other decorative materials can be used, but they are not necessary.

A sponge filter can operate in very shallow water, making it useful in small betta display tanks and tanks with fry.

The best water quality produces the best and brightest colors in bettas. Even the best genetics cannot overcome polluted water.

If a betta seems to be listless even if these conditions are given, adding salt to the water at the rate of a tablespoon for each gallon of water can help. The salt should be non-iodized. Give a water change two or three days later and repeat the salt treatment as necessary. Be watchful for signs of disease.

Water Temperatures

When a betta is listless, drab, or dark-looking and keeps his fins closed all the time, it is reasonable to assume that the problem is being caused by incorrect water conditions. More often than not, the problem is specifically caused by water that is too cool. In nature bettas are found in swamps and rice paddies in countries such as Thailand where the climate is hot and moist most of the year. Even though domesticated bettas have had many changes bred into them, domestication has not changed their environmental requirements much. Therefore, bettas still need to have very warm water compared to that required by most other ornamental fishes. An aquarium constantly maintained at about 80 degrees Fahrenheit is a bit too warm for most aquarium fishes, but not for bettas, for which it is about ideal. (Some keepers say that 80 degrees causes bettas to age too fast, so they prefer temperatures around 74 to 78 degrees.)

Now it becomes obvious why it is so difficult to keep bettas in showy condition in small, unheated bowls or brandy snifters. At a room temperature of 70 degrees, a betta will just lie on the bottom or hide behind the filter. At that temperature it will be very lethargic and will not feed very enthusiastically. In fact, bettas often starve to death at 70 degrees no matter what kind or how much food is offered. However, gradually raise the water temperature to 80 degrees and a remarkable transformation takes place. That dark blob from the bottom of the tank suddenly comes to life. It begins to swim actively with its fins open, its colors lighten and brighten to a spectacular brilliance (especially in the male), and it becomes alert, responding quickly to all stimuli around it. It feeds almost gluttonously. The difference between a cool betta and a warm betta is so marked that once you've seen the difference you'll never again keep a betta in unheated water. Temperatures slightly above 80 serve to stimulate breeding.

Water Chemistry

Water hardness and pH, although not as critical as temperature where breeding and raising bettas are concerned, are quite important. In nature bettas are found in fairly soft waters that are neutral to slightly acidic; rarely is the water alkaline. In captivity, bettas seem to be quite flexible in their water hardness and pH requirements as long as extremes are avoided. Water having a hardness of 2 to 12 degrees (DH) and a pH near neutral (about 6.4 to 7.4) seems to be tolerated quite well. Bettas will breed successfully in ordinary tap water with a pH of 7.0 to 7.2 and a DH of 8 to 12, but some hobbyists swear by soft, acid water with a pH of 6.4 and DH of 2 to 4. There probably really is no right or wrong water composition for raising bettas as long as extremes are avoided.

Warm, Not Hot

Bettas do best between about 74 and 80 degrees Fahrenheit. Temperatures lower than this may lead to stress and diseases. Breeding often is improved by slightly higher temperatures. Avoid water over 85 degrees, especially in small containers.

Bettas are no more tolerant of pollutants such as ammonia, hydrogen sulfide, carbon dioxide, and nitrites than are any other fishes. That they are more tolerant of these pollutants is a misconception that too many hobbyists believe because they know the fish can use atmospheric oxygen. This has little to do with pollutants in the water, however, as such things as ammonia and nitrates can destroy gill membranes and even affect the labyrinth organ, making it difficult for bettas to utilize atmospheric oxygen. Excesses of pollutants in the water can put bettas under severe environmental stress, making them more susceptible to diseases such as ich, velvet, fin rot, and gill diseases than they would be in pollutant-free water.

Filtration and Aeration

Bettas need special consideration where water circulation is concerned. In nature bettas are found in swamps, rice paddies, drainage ditches, and small stagnant pools. They are obviously quite well adapted to these habitats and cannot handle swift currents or fast-moving water. For this reason aeration and filtration should be quite mild. The problem with water movement is especially difficult for domesticated bettas that have very long, flowing fins. Bettas that behave lethargically when kept under all the right conditions except water movement become active, colorful fish when the water circulation is reduced to just a bit more than a trickle.

As long as there are plenty of plants and other decorations in a community tank, bettas can be kept without much difficulty because the currents created by filters are broken by objects in the tank. If a betta is kept in a relatively barren tank, the strength of the filtration should be reduced. In other words, don't use a power filter in such a tank.

Underground filters and box filters can be used successfully in betta rearing tanks if they are properly installed. Make sure the riser tubes of these filters reach to the surface of the water; this maximizes their efficiency. Some filters have an elbow that is installed at the top of the riser tube, increasing water circulation by directing filtered water across the surface and at the same time controlling excessive turbulence that could be disturbing to bettas. If using an undergravel filter, be sure the gravel is thick enough, as there must be enough substrate to house bacterial colonies that decompose wastes. Two to three inches of gravel is sufficient.

Tanks—Large and Small

Any container in which a betta is kept can be called an aquarium. Unfortunately, male bettas, because of their long, flowing fins, seldom

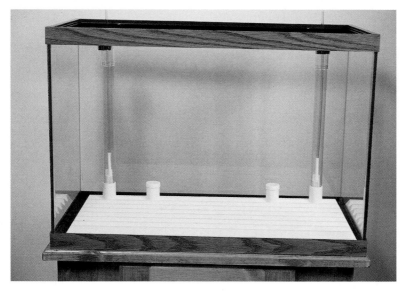

Female bettas or a single male betta can be kept in community aquaria. Larger tanks must have filters, such as the simple undergravel filter shown here.

Quick & Easy Betta Care

Flake foods of many types and qualities are available, but only the best will do for your pet. A well-balanced diet is a must for your betta.

can be kept in a community tank with active fishes such as barbs and tetras, which would continually nip at their fins and eventually stress the betta to death. Remember that male bettas exhibit aggressive behavior against males of their species and sometimes their females, but rarely against fishes of other species; they seldom even defend themselves against attacks from non-bettas. Thus a single male betta can be kept in a community aquarium only if there are no aggressive, active, or fin-nipping fishes in the tank.

Female bettas get along much better in the community tank, though they will sometimes fight with each other, resulting in split fins. Females lack the long fins of males and thus attract the attention of fewer fin-nippers and are more active and maneuverable to escape annoying neighbors.

By using dividers, (available in a pet shop) it is possible to partition a larger aquarium to hold a half dozen or more male bettas. There are many types of dividers, but generally they either allow you to

Tankmates

If you decide to keep other animals with a single male betta in a small container, restrict your choices to small, inactive species. Many hobbyists find a dwarf underwater frog or a single corydoras catfish to be a good tankmate. A single medium-sized snail will help clean the bottom. Avoid active fishes that might cause stress or damage to the betta.

run a perforated sheet to the bottom of the tank at regular intervals or to submerge rows of small cubicles in the tank, each to contain a male betta. This allows you to keep a single large aquarium, with the advantages of stable temperatures and regular filtration, which makes keeping easier and safer for the fish.

Single betta males can be kept in containers that are at least a quart in capacity and preferably a gallon or a bit more if they are not filtered. The container must be monitored for temperature (invest in

Small worms such as black worms, tubifex worms, and chopped earthworms are excellent for bringing out activity and good colors in bettas.

Quick & Easy Betta Care

Adult brine shrimp, after being washed in fresh water to remove excess salt, are a great betta food. Chemicals in their bodies increase red tones in bettas.

a good thermometer) so it is not allowed to get too hot or too cold (never outside the range of 70 to 84 degrees, preferably near 78 to 80 degrees, and fairly constant). Keep a gallon or more of water on hand airing and use it to make the water change at least every week and preferably twice a week; it should be the same temperature as the water being replaced. Use a filter if you can, and be careful if using a hood containing a light. Even a small fluorescent light bulb can produce a great amount of heat that will rapidly bring a small container of water to 90 degrees or more, killing your fish.

Though small containers such as brandy snifters are decorative and really are not harmful to a male betta, they require considerable time to maintain them properly. If time is a problem for you, it is best to invest in a small, filtered aquarium that looks just as good and requires less maintenance.

Foods and Feeding
The key to healthy bettas is a proper diet. Bettas that are fed well,

considering both quality as well as quantity, are much more resistant to diseases than are bettas raised on an unbalanced diet. In addition, well-fed bettas have much more tolerance for the occasional pollutants they may be exposed to than do malnourished bettas.

A diet consisting of only one kind of food or even just a few types is bound to cause malnutrition in fishes. Although a high-protein diet is quite important, other components are important as well. Bettas need their share of carbohydrates and fats, as well as the trace minerals and vitamins that they would get in nature. Bulk, usually vegetable fiber, has an essential role even in the diet of carnivorous fishes such as bettas and comes from the gut of insect prey as well as the chitinous shells of tiny crustaceans in the diet.

Many essential components of the betta's diet can be provided by commercially prepared dry flake or pelleted foods. Many types and brands are available at any pet shop, but some are better than others, providing a more complete regimen. Some even contain ingredients that help promote growth or better color. Some are based mostly on one type of ingredient, such as shrimp, tubifex worms, or plankton, while others are blends of these ingredients as well as vegetables. Try several brands and types to see which work best for you and your fish, and continue to vary the prepared foods on occasion. Never let your betta survive on a diet of just one item, and be sure to never overfeed, especially when keeping a betta in a small container.

Prepared betta foods also are available in the form of freeze-dried and frozen shrimp, insects, and mixtures. Freeze-dried foods are easy to use and can be stored for a long time if they are kept in airtight, moisture-proof containers. Frozen foods often include diced shrimp and clams, mosquito larvae, bloodworms and glassworms, and daphnia. All these foods, when thawed, are relished by a betta almost like living prey.

A betta needs a well-balanced diet to maintain its health and coloring. Various types of pellets and flakes are available in your local pet shop.

Almost all breeders of bettas use prepared foods, usually a meat and cereal combination. Some are cooked and some are not. Such meats as chicken liver, beef heart and liver, dog and cat foods, and fish meal have been used, often mixed with ground spinach, kale, spirulina algae, carrots, and similar vegetables. Frozen foods are chopped, scraped, melted, or fed with an eyedropper depending on their consistency and composition. Some of these products, such as beef heart mixes, may be available in the frozen food section of your pet shop.

In some betta breeding programs, live foods sometimes are a major part of the diet. Though some hobbyists have had success breeding bettas without ever using live foods, more often than not the bigger, more colorful, long-finned specimens result from a diet with live foods used at least as a supplement to a diet of prepared and frozen foods. Hobbyists can use live foods available at many larger pet shops and from dealers on the Internet. Common live foods include whiteworms and microworms often fed to fry, vestigial-winged fruitflies, mosquito larvae, bloodworms (larvae of a midge, a type of fly), glassworms (larvae of a fly related to the mosquito), and daphnia (a tiny crustacean that often appears orange-red when concentrated). These may be available seasonally or all year from dealers maintaining cultures.

Brine shrimp, both as the tiny larvae (nauplii) and the larger adults, often are fed to bettas as a supplement. Brine shrimp can be purchased in the frozen or freeze-dried form, as the main ingredient of many prepared diets, living as subadults, and as eggs that can be raised in the home to provide an endless source of larvae for raising betta fry. Brine shrimp nauplii are one of the standard diets for raising bettas, and many hobbyists could not do without them.

Illnesses &
Their Treatment

The diagnosis and treatment of diseases in tropical fishes, including bettas, are still in their infancy. Much is known about some of the common fish diseases such as ich and velvet and how to treat fishes having these diseases, but many illnesses are still impossible to recognize and treat. However, more often than not good aquarium management can prevent the occurrence of diseases in the aquarium. Prevention, not treatment, is the key to good aquarium management. Prevention is far easier to enact than trying to cure a disease once it appears. Any time a fish is placed under stress, it is weakened and experiences shock to varying degrees. A stressed fish is much more susceptible to attack by disease organisms than one in good health. This is because many disease-causing organisms, from viruses to protozoans and even some worms, survive well in the aquarium over long periods without attacking fish, but they increase in numbers rapidly when conditions in the aquarium deteriorate or the fish become stressed and offer an optimal target for the organisms. Just one weakened fish can produce a bloom of disease organisms of a magnitude to cause even healthy, unstressed fishes to succumb to diseases.

Water pollution often leads to disease in bettas. So does unvarying warm water temperatures, as well as sudden changes in temperature, especially drops in temperature. A poor, unvarying diet can make a betta subject to diseases, as can any type of malnutrition.

Preventive Steps

To prevent diseases in bettas, even single males kept in small containers for long periods of time, make sure your aquarium

Fins held tightly to the body (clamped) sometimes are an indication of poor water quality or the onset of a disease. Be aware of the normal behavior of your fish to catch problems early.

This colorful female is either carrying eggs or has dropsy. Could you tell the difference? Experience makes such distinctions easier, and so does knowing each betta that you own.

keeping routine is rigidly adhered to at all times. Follow a good feeding schedule; change the water at least weekly, replacing it with chlorine-free, aged water of the same temperature as the old water. Siphon excess food and wastes from the bottom of the container daily. Learn to recognize the normal appearance and behavior of your pet so you can recognize when it is breathing too fast, becomes more listless than normal, or changes colors. Labored or rapid

Antibiotics

Some hobbyists think that antibiotics are cure alls—just add a few drops to the tank and the disease is gone in a few days; add twice as much and it disappears even faster. Unfortunately, antibiotics are tricky to use, often are restricted by law, and today no longer are effective on some common bacteria. Antibiotics do not work on viruses and seldom work on protozoans. Use antibiotics only as a last resort, and always follow instructions to the letter.

Illnesses & Their Treatment

breathing is one of the first signs of ammonia poisoning and also one of the first symptoms of bacterial gill diseases and ich. If the fish is glancing off objects (flashing), this is an attempt to scratch the itch caused by ich or velvet or even by chemicals in the water. Ragged fins could mean a dietary deficiency or a bacterial or fungal infection.

If a betta in an aquarium (usually a female) develops any unusual behaviors or abnormalities, it should immediately be isolated from other fishes to prevent spread of a disease and make it easier to observe and treat the fish. Medications should be used with great caution and discretion, because their overuse can cause severe effects, even death. Antibiotics, especially, must be used only when definitely required and used for the entire recommended course of treatment at the recommended dosages. Using antibiotics as a preventative in low dosages just increases the resistance of bacteria and protozoan parasites to the drugs and eventually makes the drugs useless in treating illnesses. Be careful when trying to use two or more medications at the same time—medications often interact (synergisms) to overwhelm a fish that is already stressed. The same applies to using medications at higher than recommended dosages—doubling a dose will not cure a disease twice as fast but could kill the betta. Use all medications with extreme care, do not over-medicate, and follow instructions exactly. Try simple remedies (salt, temperature changes, etc.) before more complicated solutions such as advanced biochemicals.

Salt

Adding a bit of non-iodized salt to the water in the betta tank often cures or at least slows the progress of disease organisms. Bettas can tolerate about a tablespoon of salt per gallon of water without undue stress. Change such salted water daily and add fresh salt after each change for up to a week.

Ich or White Spot

Ich is one of the most common and persistent diseases of tropical fishes, and few aquarists have not had to cope with it at one time or another. It is recognized by small white spots (cysts) about the size of a grain of salt on the body and especially fins of the betta. The fish glances about, trying to scratch the obviously irritating spots. Each white spot represents an encysted protozoan parasite that is or has been feeding on body fluids of the host fish. Once the feeding period is over, the cyst drops off the fish and falls to the bottom. Reproduction occurs in the cyst. About 24 hours after the cyst falls off, it breaks open and releases hundred of microscopic free-swimming parasites called tomites or swarmers. Each tomite seeks out a host upon which to feed; if it does not find a host in about two days, it dies. Otherwise it attaches, starts feeding, forms a cyst, and reproduces.

The only part of the life cycle of the ich parasite, known as *Ichthyophthirius multifiliis*, that is treatable is the free-swimming stage. The simplest method, which often works if the disease is caught early, is to raise the temperature to about 86 degrees and hold it there for up to three weeks. This water temperature is too high to allow the swarmers to attach and reproduce, and eventually all the organisms die. However, keeping a betta at 86 degrees for so long can be stressful itself, so be careful to monitor its condition at all times. Treatment with salt at one tablespoon per gallon also may be successful.

Most pet shops sell medications designed to kill the swarmer cells of ich before they attach. Often based on the dye malachite green, the medications work if used at the proper strength and for the entire treatment period, usually at least ten days and often three weeks. If you stop the treatment when cysts stop appearing, the swarmers may still be in the bottom of the container and the ich will reappear in a few days or weeks when conditions are to its liking. Always follow instructions on the bottle!

Ich Life Cycle

- Swarmer attaches to fish
- Feeds for one to two weeks
- Cyst falls to bottom
- Reproduction
- Swarmers released in 2 days
- Swarmers have 2 days to find host

Velvet

Though caused by a very different parasite, a type of microscopic alga called *Oodinium*, velvet closely resembles ich at first glance. The infected betta develops areas of yellowish granules along the back that spread over the body and fins. These granules contain the disease organism and are smaller than the cysts of ich and more widely distributed. Sometimes a fish with velvet moves with clamped fins. The spots are most visible on the clear pectoral fins (behind the head). Young bettas, from a few days to two months old, are especially susceptible to velvet, and the disease is very contagious in the rearing tank, leading to many rapid deaths. Unfortunately, the small size of the granules makes them hard to notice until the disease becomes a massive infection, so velvet must be suspected if bettas suddenly start to hold their fins clamped to the body.

Velvet is treated much like ich, with salt (one tablespoon per gallon) the preferred treatment. Make a complete water change and add the salt, repeating the change and salt in two days. Continue this until the fish acts normally and no yellowish areas can be seen, even in the pectoral fins. Pet shops carry medicines used to treat velvet that are very effective if the instructions are followed exactly.

Bacterial Fin Rot

This is a bacterial infection of the fins of a betta. It usually attacks the outer edges of the fins, especially the caudal fin. The bacteria are especially common in containers with poor water quality and wastes on the bottom, so good aquarium maintenance reduces the incidence of the disease. Young bettas also are very susceptible, and the disease spreads from fish to fish in a rearing tank. Often the caudal fin and the ventral fins turn white, stiffen, and become brittle. At this point it may be too late to treat the disease, so learn to look at your fish and notice any small changes that might indicate the disease.

The best treatment is a wide-spectrum antibiotic dissolved in the water. Your pet shop should carry a usable antibiotic in the proper concentration; be sure to use it for the entire course of treatment, not just until the fins clear, or the bacteria may develop resistance to the treatment and next time may not be killed. If caught early, sometimes a complete water change, removing all waste from the bottom, helps control the disease or eliminates it, but most of the time you will have to use an antibiotic.

Fungus Infections

Spores of fungi are always present in water, but they usually are not a problem. When a fish has a disease or a sore, however, it is weakened enough that the spores may develop into cottony growths especially obvious on the mouth and fins or on an open wound. Sometimes it looks like a raggedy white edge to the fins, like bacterial fin rot. Fungal infections should be considered warnings that your maintenance is not as good as it should be—delayed water changes, wastes on the bottom, and low temperatures all can lead to fungal growth on even a small wound such as a frayed fin.

Treatment often is time-consuming and may not work on fish that show large infected areas such as cottony tufts over the eyes or along most of the fins. First the water is changed completely and all wastes are removed. The fish is then given a salt dip. This consists of holding it in a net in a container of water with four tablespoons of non-iodized salt per gallon until it becomes stressed, often just a minute or less. Next, holding the fish in the net, swab the infected areas (but never the

Saprolegnia

Many types of fungi spend their entire lives in the water, growing from bits of decomposing waste on the bottom. They produce spores that can survive days or even months in nearly dry conditions, waiting to revive when proper growing conditions return. Most of the aquatic fungi are called saprolegnia, based on one common genus of the group. They produce the cottony white tufts that you often see on old food rotting on the bottom of the tank. Saprolegnia fungi can easily infect small wounds on bettas and grow into a major problem. Keep the tank clean at all times to prevent fungal infections.

gills or gill covers) with Mercurochrome and let it work in for 30 seconds before returning the betta to the clean water in its container. Repeat the dip daily and the swabbing every three or four days. Obviously this treatment is extremely stressful to a fish, and many do not survive. Your pet shop may have medications for fungus that will work on bettas, but some treatments may be toxic to the already stressed fish. If you can find a good antifungal medication, be sure to use it only in the recommended dosages and never exceed that dosage—most chemicals that kill fungi also can kill your bettas.

Fortunately, bettas are very hardy fish if kept correctly, and if your fish is kept in a small container that is cleaned and changed on a regular schedule you should see few or no diseases. Be sure, of course, that any new fish you purchase is free of ich and velvet when you bring it home, or you could transfer its infection to your other fish through contaminated cleaning utensils or splashed water. Above all, try to avoid stressing your pet beyond its normal limits—a few tears in a fin are normal with bettas, due to their activity, but decomposing fin edges are not.

Resources

Advanced Bettas
A message board devoted to betta keepers. Has many commercial links if your are looking for new fish.
http://groups.msn.com/AdvancedBettas

AquaBid
Buy and sell unique betta strains and other fishes
www.aquabid.com

Betta Webring
An interesting and informative commercial site.
www.bettasrus.com

California Betta Society
An active IBC chapter on the Pacific Coast
http://cbs.bettas.org

Canadian Bettas
If you're in Canada, the IBC chapter for you is Betta Breeders Canada
http://groups.yahoo.com/group/BB Canada

Delphi Betta Forum
Post your questions and get help from knowledgeable breeders.
http://forums.delphiforums.com/bettabreeders

International Betta Congress
The IBC is the dominant betta organization today, with many active chapters. Publishes an informative newsletter. A club for beginners and advanced betta keepers alike.
http://ibc.bettas.com
e-mail: bettacongress@yahoo.com

New York Area Bettas
Try the Big Apple Betta Breeders, an IBC chapter
www.babb.info

Tropical Fish Hobbyist
The oldest tropical fish magazine in the US today, it often publishes informative articles on bettas.
Tropical Fish Hobbyist
P. O. Box 427
Neptune, NJ 07754-9989
www.tfh.com

Wild Betta Species
There are no comprehensive sites on these, but try the following for bits of information.
www.wildbettas.com
http://home.c2i.net/philippi/Betta/betta.htm

Index

Photo Credits

Bob Allen, p. 5
Isabelle Francais, p. 49
O. Lucanus, p. 8
A. Lucas, pp. 27, 56
H. Mayer, p. 26
Aaron Norman, pp. 3, 7, 35, 45, 53, 57
Andre Roth, pp. 4, 11 (top), 40
Mark Smith, pp. 11 (bottom), 41, 44
Kenjiro Tanaka, pp. 1, 6, 9, 14-16, 19-21, 23-25, 30-33, 36, 37, 42, 55
E. Taylor, p. 13
M. Walls, pp. 50, 51